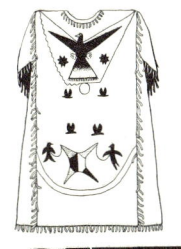

SITTING BULL

By Faith Yingling Knoop

DILLON PRESS, INC.
MINNEAPOLIS, MINNESOTA

©1974 by Dillon Press, Inc. All rights reserved

Dillon Press, Inc., 500 South Third Street
Minneapolis, Minnesota 55415

Printed in the United States of America

Library of Congress Cataloging in Publication Data

Knoop, Faith Yingling.
  Sitting Bull.
  (The Story of an American Indian)
  SUMMARY: A biography of the medicine man, artist, singer, storyteller, and warrior who was the only man ever to be chief of all the Plains Sioux.
  1. Sitting Bull, Dakota chief, 1831-1890 — Juvenile literature. [1. Sitting Bull, Dakota chief, 1831-1890. 2. Dakota Indians — Biography. 3. Indians of North America — Biography]   I. Title.
E99.D1K58   970.3   [B]   [92]   74-12015
ISBN 0-87518-065-5

ON THE COVER:
Sitting Bull as photographed by George E. Spencer at Fort Sheridan.

SITTING BULL

Sitting Bull, a Hunkpapa Sioux, grew up on the Great Plains of South Dakota. He learned to respect the customs and traditions of his people, and made his Vision Quest and danced the Sun Dance at an early age. A man of considerable talents, Sitting Bull was a singer of his own songs, a gifted orator, an artist in pictograph, and a medicine man who received visions of future events. He was also a courageous warrior, and respected leader. Sitting Bull was the only man ever to be honored as chief of all the Plains Sioux. During his adult years, he saw the takeover of the Great Plains by white settlers and soldiers. Sitting Bull resisted the white men, and participated in the Battle of the Little Big Horn on June 25, 1876.

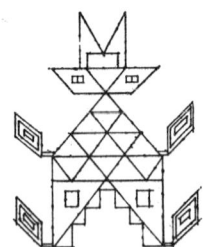

Contents

I	SLOW: AN INDIAN BOY	page 1
II	SITTING BULL IS NAMED	page 8
III	BUFFALO HUNT AND MANHOOD	page 14
IV	A STRONG HEART	page 24
V	WAR WITH PALEFACES	page 31
VI	ELECTING A CHIEF OF ALL THE PLAINS SIOUX	page 36
VII	MORE BROKEN PROMISES	page 41
VIII	CUSTER'S LAST BATTLE	page 46
IX	TRAILS TO THE FOUR WINDS	page 53
X	GHOSTS	page 64
XI	AFTER THE END	page 71

CHAPTER I

Slow: An Indian Boy

It was the summer of 1844 on the Great Plains, hunting grounds of the Sioux, the largest Indian nation on the North American continent. Once the Sioux nation with its many divisions had spread over central North America, with Sioux bands east of the Appalachian Mountains and in southern Mississippi. But now, most of the Sioux people were in the Teton or Dakota division. They were called the Plains Sioux because they lived and hunted on the Great or High Plains.

These grasslands reached from Canada in the north through the Dakotas to the south, below the Platte River in Nebraska. In the east, the hunting grounds stretched from Minnesota and the Missouri River west to Montana and Wyoming's Big Horn Mountains. Here the earth shook under countless buffalo herds. And here Sitting Bull was born.

Sitting Bull was a Hunkpapa, which was one of the seven Sioux bands. He was born near the Grand River in today's South Dakota, about 1830. Like other Sioux children, he was not given his lifelong name at birth. Most fathers would first name their sons for someone in the family, often a grandparent. Then their playmates might give them a nickname until a name had been earned by some outstanding deed. This became the lifelong name. For many years, Sitting Bull was known as Slow. His nickname was given because he was often slow to come when called and then slow to act. He had to figure out everything he did before doing it, perhaps first going to a hilltop and praying to Wakan Tanka, the Great Spirit. But once he started to do anything, Slow tore into action, and he always beat everyone in the boys' games.

In 1844, Slow was fourteen, and he already had the strength and muscles of a warrior. He seemed able to see the future, like a shaman, or medicine man. He had a voice that made people listen to his words when sung or spoken. He talked with the birds and made up his own songs to sing. He was an artist, too, and drew pictures of his father's brave deeds on his tepee walls. At ten, and without permission, he had killed a buffalo calf. Truly, his father, Jumping Bull, could be thankful for such a son.

Ever since that first buffalo hunt, Slow had found play hunts with other children boring. But he was always asked to lead them, for the younger boys looked up to him as a teacher. After the hunts, Slow would leave the younger children, for he longed to begin hunting with the men and to become a warrior.

One day, after a hunt, Slow loped to his grazing pony nearby. His father had given it to him when he was ten. As he ran, he sang his own song about his bird friend, Yellow Hammer, who had once saved his life.

That day, years before, Slow had been riding his pony near the woods of the Black Hills. At noon's heat, he lay down to nap under a shady cottonwood tree. He dreamed that a grizzly bear, most feared animal of the Hills, stood over him. The grizzly is the hardest animal to kill, and the deadliest to meet. As the bear stood over him, Slow heard in his dream a bird, a Yellow Hammer, knock twice on the tree above. "Lie still!" the knocks said.

Slow awoke, but did not open his eyes. He still seemed to feel the bear's hot breath on his face. He peered from under his lids and, sure enough, a grizzly did stand over him. Again Slow heard Yellow Hammer's warning taps, "Lie still!"

So Slow pretended to sleep on, for grizzlies were said not to attack a dead or sleeping person. After a long time, the bear turned and lumbered away.

When the grizzly was gone, Slow looked up at the bird in the tree above. Then he began to sing the song the Great Spirit put into his mouth:

Pretty bird, you pitied me.
You wished me to live longer with my people.
Oh, Bird People, from this day,
You shall always be part of my family.

Today, remembering Yellow Hammer, Slow galloped away on his pony across the Plains to a far hill. On its rounded top, Slow shaded his eyes with his flattened hand. Yes, they were there — distant smoke towers rising from the earth. He gave a great yell of joy, and turned back. Soon the Hunkpapas must war against the Crows trespassing on Hunkpapa land. Slow had decided he would join the warriors in the attack. He was not a child anymore.

Once in camp, Slow hurried to his own tepee. His mother, Her Holy Door, was boiling deer stew in a bag made from a buffalo's paunch. The bag hung from a tripod over the fire before the tepee. Stew in the bag was kept warm by putting hot stones in with the meat. Jumping Bull had eaten and joined older men sitting on the ground in a circle nearby.

"The boys are listening to the story of the Little People," Slow's mother said.

Slow smiled. "I have heard the story many times," he answered. "I will eat now."

Her Holy Door took a turtleback plate and a buffalo-horn ladle. She dished up a serving of the deer meat and handed it to Slow, who ate hungrily. Then he bounded away to the fire where the grandfather told stories about mice, the Little People. This would be the last time for him to sit with the children, he thought. Tomorrow he would do man's work.

At first, as always, the grandfather was telling of the Sioux. "Our people live in the beautiful, forested Black Hills, our holy mountains. The Great Spirit, Wakan Tanka, gave them to us, his favorite tribe, to hold forever. We also dwell in the Badlands. They are bare and rocky, and have old, pink-gray ridges cut up with narrow canyons. They protect our hunting grounds from enemies, who become lost in the rocks and caves.

"And best of all," the old man went on, "the Sioux nation holds the Great Plains, the grasslands where the buffalo live. For the buffalo give us everything we need — meat for food; hides for tents, boats, and clothes; bones for tools; sinews for string."

All this the boys had heard often before. Gall, who was Slow's adopted brother, wanted to get on with the story of the Little People. "All animals are good for us," he put in. "But what good are Little People, anyway? They are not

The Black Hills (above) and the Badlands of South Dakota

even good to eat. Mice are good for nothing. They only steal the food we store in caves."

The grandfather shook his head. "Wakan Tanka has a reason for all his beings. The Little People are Moon Nibblers who live in the sky. When the moon is full, the Little People always come out and dance. Then they begin to nibble the moon away. Sometimes they nibble too much and make holes in the moon. Then they are cast down from the sky. They know some magic, but they know no way to live on earth except by nibbling."

The storyteller added, "We need Moon Nibblers. Without them, the full moon would shine every night. We would not sleep well. And we could not raid enemy camps without being seen."

During the story, Slow sat behind the circle, only half listening. Earlier that day, he had heard men planning a war party for tomorrow. Unknown to them, Slow, too, would be with them. He had a plan, and he felt that Wakan Tanka had given him his blessing.

Suddenly Slow sat up straight. For there came to the campfire another older man, Elk Horn, who had just returned from a visit toward the Rising Sun. "I have something to tell," Elk Horn began. Now Slow listened hard.

The boys said softly, "Washtay! — Good!"

"I saw many white men on my journey," Elk Horn began. "They came to the camp I visited and stared at everyone. They were heading for the setting sun. These men are something like the trappers we have seen, but whiter. They wear very tight clothes that cover them all over, even on hot days. And they walk like this, in big, hard moccasins."

Elk Horn waddled across the circle with short steps, toes

7 SLOW: AN INDIAN BOY

pointing out. The boys howled with laughter. How could one get anywhere unless he pointed his toes straight ahead?

"These white men are said to live in big ugly boxes. They have no comfortable tepees, warm in winter and cool in summer when the sides are rolled up to catch the breezes. They do not know how to hunt with arrows. But they have one fearful thing — a thunder stick. It is a hollow stick that shoots pebbles of death from its mouth. These pebbles kill animals and can kill persons, too."

The speaker drew a deep breath. "We must have nothing to do with such beings, because of the thunder stick," he went on. "They make up stories, too. They say that millions of their kind live beyond the sunrise and wish to follow them to the sunset. But the land of the Hunkpapas was given us by Wakan Tanka himself, and cannot belong to white men." As Slow listened, he felt a sudden cold chill.

Stories were over. The boys ran to their tepees while Slow followed slowly, thinking. He had seen a few whites — trappers who came to trade knives, cloth, and beads for Hunkpapa furs. Their faces and chests were hairy, and this seemed strange to the smooth-skinned Indians. But their skins were not much lighter than that of the Indians, and they usually had Indian wives. Until now, Slow had thought little about these men.

The boy felt in his heart that Wakan Tanka had chosen him to be a leader of his people someday. If this were true, he must remember Elk Horn's words. He would forbid white men and their thunder sticks to enter the buffalo plains. Then the strangers would go back to their boxes in the land of the rising sun. Or would they?

CHAPTER II

Sitting Bull Is Named

That night, Slow hardly slept at all. He knew that the men planned to set out before dawn. Good Voiced Elk was the leader of the war party. Slow's father, Jumping Bull, was next in charge. In spite of the bright moonlight, they must punish the Crows who were now on Hunkpapa land stealing their horses.

At last Slow heard someone tiptoe to his tepee and give a low owl hoot. He heard his father move quietly to the tepee's flap opening. Slow's mother followed, to bid her husband good-bye and good luck. Slow waited until Her Holy Door crept back to her soft bed of buffalo skins on willow branches. Then Slow rolled off his own buffalo cot, on the other side of the tepee. The tent's buffalo hide walls were partly rolled up, for air. Slow crept outside, beneath the tepee wall. His mother would not miss him until sunrise. Then she would be proud.

Slow wore only his breechcloth and moccasins, and carried a coup stick. He had made the coup stick himself, and hidden it under his cot. He had peeled the bark from a straight branch of the cottonwood tree and had fastened a tuft of feathers at the end of the stick, which was longer than he was tall. A coup stick was more important to him

9 SITTING BULL IS NAMED

today than weapons, for he was determined to count coup in battle.

In Sioux battles, each warrior tried to count coup on as many enemies as possible. Coup (pronounced "coo") was the French word for "strike" or "hit." The winners in battles were those who counted coup on the most enemies, by hitting them with the coup sticks or even with their hands. It was more worthy to count coup on a live enemy than to kill one and then count coup. Up to three warriors might count coup by hitting the same foe. Each coup he counted gave a warrior the right to wear another feather in his headband. It was almost unheard of for a fourteen-year-old boy to count coup.

Now Slow heard the war party's light footsteps moving toward the war horses tied beside the camp. They must be silent, for Crow scouts might lie within hearing distance and race home to report a possible attack. Dogs barked, but that meant nothing, because they barked at anything, day and night.

Slow crept through the shadows behind the war party. When the warriors had mounted and trotted away in the night, he found his pony and followed slowly. He must keep far enough behind the men not to be seen by them, but close enough to join them for the attack.

The full moon might help, after all, in surprising the enemy. Crows would not expect the Sioux to ride out in moonlight. Finally the night dimmed into darkness and the eastern sky grew pink. As the sun rose, Slow stopped to face and salute it, and he saw the distant shadow of the war party do the same. Soon all moved on.

Slow shivered a little in the cold dawn and almost wished

he had worn his buckskin shirt and breeches. But excitement soon warmed him.

Low hills and clumps of bushes dotted the plain, fragrant with its sagebrush. Slow grew bolder, urging his pony into a gallop toward the men. When they disappeared into a thicket, he galloped after them at full speed. He knew that they were pulling off their shirts and long leather pants, getting ready for battle. He must join them now. Would they send him back, like a baby?

The sun beamed on earth and men. Panting, Slow galloped boldly into the thicket and pulled up his pony. No one paid any attention to him. The men, now in breechcloths and moccasins, were painting themselves for war. Each had already tied his long, black hair into a war knot above his forehead. Slow jumped to the ground. He sidled toward the buffalo-skin bag holding red paint made from red earth. His father finished painting himself and tossed his paint stick into the bag. Slow took it out and colored himself like the men, with streaks on his face, neck, arms, body, and legs. Still no one spoke to him. He looked at his father. Jumping Bull whispered, "Do what is brave, my son," and turned away. Slow thought he saw pride in his father's eyes.

The Plains Indians' warfare was nothing like white men's wars where armies of soldiers shot at other armies. Indian war parties were often small, like this one of about twenty-five men. Once the war party met the enemy, each brave fought for himself, counting coup if he could, on one enemy after another. Returning home, each told of his own victories.

Now the warriors mounted their horses. Slow jumped

upon his pony's back, holding his coup stick tightly. In their belts or tied on their horses the warriors carried coup sticks, spears, shields, bows, knives, and clubs. Arrows were in quivers strapped across their shoulders. Plains Indians did not need to use their horses' reins all the time, so their hands were free to aim their weapons. The riders sat their mounts as if part of them. They guided with their knees, heels, and a slight shifting of their bodies. In battle they often slid over on the sides of their horses to shoot under the horses' heads.

Suddenly the warriors screeched their war cry, "Hoka Hey!" They slapped their open mouths with their hands, screaming, "Ha! Ha! Ha!" Slow yelled, too, as he saw a Crow war party galloping toward him. He prayed Wakan Tanka would make him brave. The sweat of excitement broke out on his forehead.

The two parties clashed head on. Slow's eyes darted in all directions. He saw a Crow wheel his horse suddenly to attack a Hunkpapa. The Crow either did not see Slow, or thought the young boy was not worth noticing. Slow raced his pony toward the Crow. Then the boy, armed only with his coup stick, ran it full force into the enemy's side. Taken by surprise, the Crow was caught off balance and fell to the ground. Slow remembered to shout as he counted coup, "I, son of Jumping Bull, count coup!"

The battle was soon over; the crows, losing heart, turned and fled. The Hunkpapas began to chant victory songs. Jumping Bull chanted loudest of all, "My son counted coup. We shall celebrate. He is a man!"

Before the celebration the next day, Slow rode to the nearest hill to thank Wakan Tanka for his victory.

*A hill where Sitting Bull
is known to have prayed to Wakan Tanka*

That night there was a feast never to be forgotten in the Hunkpapa camp. Everyone ate pemmican — dried buffalo meat boiled in buffalo paunches and kept hot with the hot stones. There was wasna — ground buffalo meat, dried and mixed with wild berries and marrow. And there were roast fish, bear, rabbit, and squirrel meat, fresh choke cherries, and wild turnips.

Finally came Jumping Bull's important announcement. "My son has his life's name," he said. "The buffalo god himself, who came in the form of a talking buffalo bull, once told me of four names he dreamed for my family, the family of the buffalo bull. I am Jumping Bull. My only son is Sitting Bull. Others in my family will be given the other two names when they have done deeds of worth." (In later years, Jumping Bull would give the names of One Bull and White Bull to his grandsons, sons of his oldest

13 SITTING BULL IS NAMED

daughter, Pretty Feather. Sitting Bull's two nephews would become his great warrior helpers.)

Now the shaman presented Sitting Bull with a gray eagle feather for his first coup. The feather in its band was placed on Sitting Bull's head like a crown. Her Holy Door gave him a buffalo-skin bag to keep it in when it was not being worn.

There followed the victory dance around the campfire by the men of yesterday's war party. Sitting Bull joined proudly in his first such dance. To the beat of the tom-tom and the clapping of hands, they swayed and stomped, prancing, twirling, clapping, pounding heels to earth — thud, thud, thud, thud. It was not only a dance to thank Wakan Tanka for victory, but also to ask him for further protection.

They danced until, worn out, they threw themselves to the ground, panting and happy. The shaman again thanked Wakan Tanka that no Hunkpapas had been killed in yesterday's battle. If any had died, this victory feast would not have been held until after four days of mourning for the dead. At last, all settled down to hear the shaman's stories of the Sioux.

When all was over, Sitting Bull drew a deep breath. He had done a man's job at fourteen. He had counted coup. But he had other tests to win in order to become a leader. He must endure the Vision Quest and the Sun Dance. Only then could he become a Strong Heart, one of his tribe's ruling warrior society devoted to honor and courage. Once a Strong Heart, he might become a war chief or a shaman. The name of Sitting Bull then would be known far and wide for its power and good leadership.

CHAPTER III

Buffalo Hunt and Manhood

Sitting Bull could now sit with the men in councils, though he must only listen, not take part. Jumping Bull had given his son men's weapons at once, and taught him to use them. Sitting Bull now had his own bow and arrows tipped with sharp stones. He had a spear, a knife, a heavy club of buffalo bone and stone, and a shield of buffalo hide. He practiced every day with his new warriors' weapons.

It was early fall, Moon of Falling Leaves, the best time for buffalo hunting. The great bison were fat from summer grazing. Their shaggy hair had shed, making the hides easy to cure and scrape for leather. Scouts had been sent out to find the herd closest to the Hunkpapa summer camp. Sitting Bull could hardly wait to go on his first real buffalo hunt.

Suddenly at sunrise one day, a shout went up from the camp. "The scouts signal on the western hill!"

Sitting Bull ran to an open place and squinted toward the hill. Sure enough, a smoke signal arose from the hilltop. It was a burning pile of buffalo chips, he knew. He saw the tiny figure of a scout kick the chips in four directions to show that buffalo were nearby.

15 BUFFALO HUNT AND MANHOOD

Scout Brave Bear soon galloped into camp, crying out, "Buffalo! A herd beyond the hill of tall fir trees!" A short council was held. The head councillor smoked a few puffs on his red clay pipe. He touched it to the ground, pointed it to the sky, and then to the four corners of the earth. And everyone hurried to his or her own task in moving camp toward the herd.

Women pulled down their tepees and rolled up the buffalo-hide sides to be carried away. Willow beds were packed up, along with their warm buffalo-robe covers. Horn and stone dishes, bone knives and tools were packed into buffalo-hide bags. Then the great bundles were tied onto ponies' backs or onto travois, which were sleds with long poles for runners, to be dragged over the ground by the ponies. The women worked like whirlwinds, each eager to be the first to finish her packing, ready to go.

A Sioux camp

Dogs barked and got into everyone's way. Some of the larger trained dogs had travois harnessed to them, too, to drag in the line of moving Hunkpapas. Before the Sioux had horses, they had used dogs to pull travois.

The whole process of packing often took less than a half-hour. Soon the long line of horses and ponies carrying Hunkpapas and all their belongings set out across the grassy prairie. Mothers rode with young babies on their backs. Older babies were held in front, and larger children loved to ride on the travois pulled by ponies. By the age of ten, most boys rode their own ponies.

The scouts led the way. Warriors urged their horses back and forth beside the line, protecting the caravan. Others rode behind, to check on everyone's safety. All were happy to travel again, and were excited by thought of fresh buffalo meat.

Sitting Bull would have liked to gallop far ahead, as fast as his new bay horse could run. But he must march with the band on guard. So, to while away the time, he practiced his horsemanship. He rolled off his horse as it ran, caught up, and sprang from the ground to its back. He hung by his feet first on one side, then the other. Or he slid from one side of the horse to the other, to ride hanging on with one heel to the hide rope around the horse's neck. People paid him little attention. Everyone knew that Sitting Bull was becoming the best young horseman in camp. He never walked when he could ride. And already he was becoming bowlegged from riding so much, before he was full grown.

As they neared the buffalo herd, the scouts quieted the people. They must not go too close to the herd or the animals would be scared away. The people looked for a level spot near running water, a place to set up camp.

It was soon found. Everyone dismounted and went to work. Camp was put up almost as quickly as it had been pulled down. The leaders' tepees in the center were surrounded by a circle of tepees all opening toward the east. Boys helped the squaws set up the three or four main tepee poles and fasten the tent skins around them. Then they climbed up to fix extra sticks at the top hole to carry away smoke from the fires inside. Everyone's belongings were set neatly around the tepee's inside wall. Buffalo rugs covered each tepee floor around the central fire. Cots or beds were laid and made up. Finally the women made outdoor fireplaces for cooking in good weather. The dogs were tied to trees so they couldn't run off and scare the buffalo. Now the camp was ready for the hunt and all the work to follow.

Sitting Bull slept lightly that night, waiting for the hunt. At last it was time to greet the sunrise. Then Sitting Bull galloped away with the men.

Soon they saw the buffalo herd just over the hill. It was a large herd, and the animals were well fed. Bull lookouts stood guarding it on each side. The hunters drew near the huge beasts as quietly as possible, moving against the wind so the herd would not detect the human smell. But the lookout bulls sensed danger. They began to paw the earth and bellow. The herd, uneasy, began to mill about, before the enemy was in sight. Dust rising from the herd almost hid the buffalo from the men.

Then the hunters, no longer unseen, pounded toward the great animals, yelling, "Hi! Yi! Yi!" The Indians galloped alongside the herd and began to find targets for their arrows. The milling buffalo crowded together in frenzy. The Indians watched carefully that the whole herd did not begin to move in one direction. A stampede could carry them all away, and trample the hunters. Leaders in such a movement were picked off at once.

Sitting Bull's eyes were on a great buffalo bull edging away from the herd. It looked at the boy and started toward him. Sitting Bull raised his bow, pointing his arrow at the red-eyed beast. The bull fell, rose to its feet, staggered and fell again. Before he shouted his victory, Sitting Bull remembered to say to the dead bull, "Grandfather, our children are hungry. You were made for our food. So I must kill you."

The herd moved on. Sitting Bull pulled his skinning knife from his belt. His uncle, Four Horns, galloped up to him. "I will show you the best way to skin it," he said.

That night there was great rejoicing in the Hunkpapa camp. Once more, their living was sure. The women went to work drying the hides and scraping off the hair for leather clothes and bags. They dried strips of meat on racks beside their tepees. Later they would make pemmican and wasna from the dried meat, to store in skins for winter. And of course they boiled the best fresh meat over the fires. The buffalo's hump was thought to have the most delicious meat, so the hunters were given the hump meat to feast upon.

Not a bit of the buffalo was wasted. Clothes, bedding, rugs, horses' gear, skin boats, stomach bags, horn spoons, cups and decorations, sinews for bow strings, thread and rope — all these things must now be made. Women would be busy with these tasks all winter long. Blood made red

19 BUFFALO HUNT AND MANHOOD

paint, as did the tallow mixed with ocher. The buffalo hair stuffed pillows and saddles. And the buffalo droppings dried into chips for fuel in the Plains where wood was scarce. The buffalo gave life itself to the Sioux.

After the hunt, Sitting Bull told his father, "Now I am ready for the Vision Quest. I have counted coup. I have killed a buffalo bull."

Jumping Bull nodded. "Yes, you are ready, my son," he answered. "I will talk with the shaman tomorrow."

The Vision Quest, or dream seeking, was the next step toward full manhood. First, a boy would be taught his tribe's history and beliefs by the shaman or medicine man. Then he must build a tiny sweat lodge in the ground, where he would stay alone for three days and nights without food or water, seeking the vision sent by Wakan Tanka himself. Upon seeing the vision, the boy would report it to the shaman, who would decide if the test had been passed.

So Sitting Bull moved from his parents' tepee to that of Moon Dreamer, the shaman. For a month the shaman taught him the history of Wakan Tanka's care for the Hunkpapas and all the Sioux. With no written language, the Indians' stories must be told and retold by the wise men. Sitting Bull listened and remembered everything.

At the end of the month, Moon Dreamer and Sitting Bull rode their horses to a nearby hill and stopped beside a running creek. Here they dug a shallow hole for a sweat lodge and lined it with sage, Wakan Tanka's sacred herb. Curved willow poles were arched over the hole and covered with buffalo robes. A pole was set up before the lodge and it was topped with a bundle of sage, some feathers, and a piece of red cloth. No visitors must come here.

Next, a fire was built between lodge and stream. Rocks were heated in the flame, then rolled to the lodge. Sitting Bull crept inside, beside the hot rocks. Then he was handed ladles of cold water. He threw the water over the stones until steam filled the cave-like space. Soon sweat poured from him. The shaman called him to come out, and Sitting Bull ran to the cold creek and dived into the icy water. Shivering, he returned to the sweat lodge. The shaman rode away, leading Sitting Bull's horse.

Alone, naked, with no food or weapon, Sitting Bull must stay at the lodge for three days and nights. During all of the first day he stood turning his face toward the sun in its daily journey across the sky. No vision came. After sunset he stumbled weakly back into his lodge to sleep.

The second day dawned and passed like the first. Weaker than before, the boy crept to the lodge at nightfall, still without a vision. "Tomorrow," he whispered, "tomorrow, Wakan Tanka, I pray for my Great Vision."

On the third day, Sitting Bull, standing in the sun, felt his legs tremble with weakness. But his eyes followed the sun's journey as before. It rose high in the heavens and began to descend. Sitting Bull was near panic when it dropped low in the sky. Was he to have no vision? "Wakan Tanka," he called in a thin voice, "Come to me!"

And then, in the third glowing red sunset beyond the Plains, Sitting Bull's prayer was answered. A great light shone around him. Music filled the air and in the light a beautiful cloudlike Being appeared for only a moment. Then the light faded and the music ceased. Sitting Bull fell to the earth, stunned. He felt that he would never be the same again.

21 BUFFALO HUNT AND MANHOOD

The Indian boy, weak and cold, walked back to camp, to the shaman's tepee. When he told his vision, Moon Dreamer smoked his pipe in silence for a long time. Sitting Bull waited uneasily. Had his vision not been enough? He had heard of men to whom a bird or beast appeared in the Vision Quest. But his bird, Yellow Hammer, had already spoken to him. Should he have talked with the Being he had seen? Was his experience too short to be a true vision?

At last Moon Dreamer began to speak. "You are indeed blessed," he said slowly. "You have been close to the Spirit of Wakan Tanka himself. You are chosen to be a leader of your people who will follow you as long as you follow Wakan Tanka." The shaman gave the boy soup, returned his horse, and sent him home.

There was still one more test of manhood before Sitting Bull could become a member of the Strong Heart Society. He must dance the Sun Dance. This ceremony took place only once a year, in early summer. It was the most important celebration of the year, with other Sioux tribes gathering for the worship of the Sun. This would be a severe test, and when Her Holy Door heard that Sitting Bull wanted to dance at the next Sun Dance, she cried aloud. Even Jumping Bull asked his son if he should not wait another year.

But Sitting Bull replied, "I have seen the Vision. I am ready to sacrifice my body to Wakan Tanka. He will help me bear the torture, so you will not be ashamed of me. When it is over, I will know I am really one with Wakan Tanka, and will always be brave in battle and blessed by the Great Spirit."

The tribes' tepees were set up in a huge circle around the Sun Dance center, but before the celebration could take place, there were many days of preparation. Each night drums pounded and eagle-bone whistles tooted for tribal dances. A tall, straight cottonwood tree was chosen as the sacred pole to be set up in the Sun Dance circle. Its limbs were cut off, its bark was peeled, and it was painted with red stripes. Great figures of an Indian and a buffalo were placed on a long, heavy crossbar fastened near the pole's top. From the crossbar dangled four pairs of rawhide thongs.

When all was ready, the tribes gathered at sunrise to sing and chant and watch Sitting Bull and three other young men dance their first Sun Dance. The four dancers were painted as for battle, their hair was loosened to the winds, and they wore only breechcloths. An eagle-bone whistle hung around the neck of each. Sitting Bull offered to be the first sacrifice.

The boy faced the east, danced to the sun, and then lay down on his back in the circle. The shaman placed a stick between his jaws to bite on, in order to ease the pain he was to bear. Then the shaman used a heavy bone awl to pierce the flesh on either side of Sitting Bull's chest. Next, a smooth stick was stuck through the wounds from one side to the other, like a skewer. A hanging thong was tied to each end of the stick, Sitting Bull was helped to his feet, and the Indians shouted, "Dance, Sitting Bull, dance!"

With blood streaming down his body from the chest skewer, Sitting Bull dazedly began to shuffle his feet. He must dance until he had pulled the skewer out through his flesh, and was free of the thongs.

When all the dancers were moving, the women ran to the dancers with cups of water. They washed blood away with healing sage and danced beside the young men. As they all danced, some boys and men jeered at the youths, "You cry like squaws! You cannot do it! You are cowards!" For if any fainted or begged to be cut down, he would be called a coward forever after.

Sitting Bull blew his eagle-bone whistle in defiance, and cried, "I laugh at pain. I have counted coup and killed bear and buffalo." Then he prayed to win in battles always.

At last, after hours that seemed like days, the wooden skewer tore through Sitting Bull's flesh. One by one the dancers all pulled free. They dropped to the ground to be helped to their feet by a shaman who washed the wounds and treated them with sage. And as each one staggered to his feet, he was greeted by cheers and drumming. Sitting Bull was given the most cheers of all, for he was the youngest hero.

After a rest, all the dancers joined with other warriors who had gone through the sacrifice and together they danced the Sun Dance in the Sun circle. Sitting Bull's wounds would soon heal, he knew, leaving scars he would be proud to show, all his life.

Years later, the United States government would forbid the Sioux Sun Dance torture forever. As for the Hunkpapas, they thanked Wakan Tanka for sending them Sitting Bull to be their leader in years to come. Now Sitting Bull was a man.

CHAPTER IV

A Strong Heart

Sitting Bull was now full grown. He was tall, but his bow legs kept him under the six feet of many Sioux warriors. He was very broad and powerful, with wide shoulders and big muscular arms. His wide face with its down-turned mouth had a stern expression except when he smiled, as he often did, at children whom he loved. Then his deep-set brown eyes twinkled.

Sitting Bull was now becoming a shaman or medicine man. Before any important battle he rode alone to the hills to pray for success. Then, with Wakan Tanka's help, he was sure of winning, and it seemed that he was able to foretell the future. Sometimes Sitting Bull would make up songs, singing them in a strong voice. And he was a good speaker, swaying his audience with his words. His teacher, the shaman Moon Dreamer, boasted that Wakan Tanka himself had sent Sitting Bull to the Sioux.

The warrior society of the Strong Hearts invited Sitting Bull to join them. The members of this important society had to swear to four ideals: bravery, generosity, honor, and wisdom. Once a member, Sitting Bull earned one honor after another among these finest young men of the Sioux.

Strong Hearts wore red sashes into battle. The sash was

a long strip of red cloth about a foot wide. The banner was hung over one shoulder, and it trailed the ground behind the warrior as he rode his horse into battle. When he took a stand against an enemy he cast a spear into the sash end, pinning it to the ground. This was a reminder that no Strong Heart ever tore the sash to run away from an enemy. For a Strong Heart must die before he would retreat.

With the sash, Sitting Bull, like the others, wore a tight cap covered with cut crow's feathers. Two short black buffalo horns stood on the cap, sticking up over each ear. White ermine fur streamers flew from the back of the cap. When Strong Hearts galloped to battle, they were enough to frighten every enemy. Red sashes and white streamers flew out behind them like pennants of danger, and black-horned caps topped their fierce faces. They sang or shouted Strong Heart songs, such as:

> Friends, whoever runs away
> Is not admitted.

Before long, Sitting Bull had worked up into the inner circle or leading group of the Strong Hearts, called the Midnight Strong Hearts. Their secret meetings were held at midnight.

Jumping Bull gave his son his finest war horse, a strong, black animal as brave as its new owner. The horse carried his master into the thick of every fight. Finally, Sitting Bull was chosen to be the leader of the Strong Hearts.

Indian battles were becoming more deadly, for white traders were exchanging Indian furs for guns. Every summer there were big trading fairs in Indian country. The warriors brought their whole families to the fairs, along with buffalo hides, beaver fur, bear, fox, and coonskin hides. At first the Indians wanted in exchange only beads, red cloth, tiny mirrors, buttons, and other trinkets. But when they saw what the whites' thunder sticks could do to animals and foes, they wanted guns in trade. So Sitting Bull and the other Strong Hearts soon had rifles to use in battle.

One day the Strong Hearts attacked an enemy camp of Hohe Indians. They wiped out one family except for its eleven-year-old son. This boy, instead of running and trying to hide, faced the Hunkpapa warriors with his small bow and arrow, daring them to kill him. As a Hunkpapa raised his spear, Sitting Bull held up his hand. "Do not hurt him," he ordered. "He is too brave to die."

*Sitting Bull
with unidentified women*

27 A STRONG HEART

The Hunkpapas growled in anger. "He must die," they said. "If you save him now, he will turn against us and try to kill us."

"Not so," Sitting Bull answered quietly. "I am adopting him as my brother. I shall call him Stays-Back until he earns another name."

This was the first of many brave foes Sitting Bull saved and then adopted. Stays-Back became the most loyal of all, the most like Sitting Bull himself. After Sitting Bull's father, Jumping Bull, was killed in battle, Stays-Back was renamed Jumping Bull as a tribute to his achievements as a warrior.

One night the Hunkpapas again captured many Crow horses and were leading them away at dawn. Then suddenly the Crow war cry screeched out behind them — "Yip, yip, yip!" followed by "Ploo! Ploo!" a sound made through loosely closed lips, like a horse's neigh. The Hunkpapas, singing the Strong Heart song, at once turned to meet the Crow's charge. Sitting Bull leaped from his horse, making for the Crow chief. Facing him, Sitting Bull dropped to one knee, behind his shield. He aimed his gun at the chief.

But the Crow fired first. The bullet slanted through the shield to hit Sitting Bull's left foot just as he fired. Then Sitting Bull's one shot killed the chief. Sitting Bull limped to count coup on him, and mounted his horse, singing the victory song. At their chief's death the Crow war party fled.

Sitting Bull's foot had been hit beneath its toes, through the sole to the heel. Back in camp, it was treated with sage and then bandaged. But the sole pulled up and never was flat again. For the rest of his life, Sitting Bull walked with a limp. But it was a proud limp, for it reminded others of his courage in the Crow battle. That story was told over and over again.

The Sioux were learning that their buffalo-hide shields, round like the sun, moon, and earth, were useless against guns. Bullets pierced them, and the shields themselves gave a better target to the enemy than no shield at all. But Sitting Bull kept this shield, though useless, in memory of that coup.

One June the Hunkpapas were breaking camp to move northwest from the Cannonball River into the Black Hills. As the long Hunkpapa line set out, a large band of Crow warriors suddenly fell upon them. The ground thundered beneath the war horses' hooves. The long war bonnet of the new Crow chief trailed behind him in a stream of color. Screaming war whoops, the attacking Crows broke through the Hunkpapa line, first cutting down a boy guard.

For a few moments all was confused among the Hunkpapas, before the warriors grouped together to meet the attack. Then again they made for the Crow chief and unhorsed him. Disgraced, the chief wailed and cried until cut down. Once more, at the loss of their chief, most Crows ran away.

One brave Crow on horseback stayed, challenging any Hunkpapa to meet him in a hand-to-hand fight. Jumping Bull, old as he was, jumped from his horse and ran toward the Crow. The Crow also leaped from his horse, shooting his last arrow at Jumping Bull and wounding him in the shoulder. Then the Crow seized his knife to stab the old man. Jumping Bull reached for his knife, too. But his knife belt had twisted around his waist. He had to fumble behind his back to get it. Before he could draw his knife, the Crow stabbed him again and again. Jumping Bull fell dead before Sitting Bull and the Strong Hearts knew what was happening.

When Sitting Bull rode up, he was too late to save his father. But he pursued the fleeing Crow and killed him. The Strong Hearts joined in chasing the other Crows, killing ten. Finally, Sitting Bull returned to the Hunkpapa line, wailing the Strong Heart death song for his father:

> Friends,
> Jumping Bull,
> Friends,
> Returns not.

The next four days of mourning for Jumping Bull were followed by the victory dance. The Hunkpapas spoke of the cowardice of the dead Crow chief.

Meanwhile, Sitting Bull prayed to Wakan Tanka about the whites trespassing on his land. Ever since he could remember, one of the greatest trade fairs had been held yearly at the meeting of the Laramie and North Platte rivers at Fort Laramie, in southwest Wyoming. The fort had been built by white fur traders. But in 1849, when Sitting Bull was nineteen, the United States had bought the fort to use as an army post. United States soldiers were stationed there to protect the wagon trains of settlers going west.

After 1849 the white men came in greater numbers than ever, to seek their fortunes in the newly discovered gold fields of California. Their great white covered wagons followed each other through the heart of the Indians' best hunting grounds. The settlers killed the Indians' game, or scared it away. Buffalo were growing scarce on the Plains and the Indians knew but one way to protect their land. They shot and killed strangers just as they would have driven off enemy Indians.

Then there came bluecoat soldiers who fought back with better rifles than those the Indians had. The soldiers also used great wagon guns that spit out huge balls, mowing down many Indians at once. How would this problem end?

In 1851, all Indian tribes were invited to a great council at Fort Laramie to meet white leaders for a peace treaty. Sitting Bull, only twenty-one, advised the Sioux against agreeing to anything. "Have nothing to do with white men," he said. "There is still good hunting between the Black Hills and Big Horn Mountains. Whites will never go into the Hills given the Sioux by Wakan Tanka."

The white officers at the Laramie meeting set up an Indian of their choosing to be chief of all Indians and sign their treaty. The treaty said that both sides promised to make a lasting peace. The Indians were to allow whites to follow certain trails through their lands. The whites would pay them each year in trade goods for this right.

When the council was over, the Indians laughed among themselves at the whites' strange ideas of naming a "paper chief" whom few Indians knew. The treaty itself became a scrap of paper, ignored by both sides. The white men went on building more forts, while Sitting Bull continued as leader of the Strong Hearts and tried to keep his people in the Black Hill country north of most covered wagon trails.

CHAPTER V

War with Palefaces

The white men kept on pouring through Sioux land. Their strange ways puzzled and sometimes amused the Indians. Lone riders began to tear back and forth on fast ponies over the vast Plains. They carried only scraps of paper with bird tracks on them, but these scraps seemed to have some magic meaning to the people receiving them.

Next, larger wagons appeared, ones even bigger than the covered wagons, and with many seats. They rolled along the covered wagon trails, taking people west. More forts went up, with soldiers to protect the pony express riders, the covered wagons, and the stagecoaches.

In time, the white men began setting up tall, dead tree trunks along the trails. They fastened heavy strings to the trees' straight, top branches. Sometimes the strings would buzz and sing. They sang songs to the others along the line, carrying messages faster than the fastest pony.

But for all their fantastic tricks, the white men were stupid when making war, the Indians thought. "They stand still in rows, waiting to be shot down," Sitting Bull would say. "When they fall, their comrades pay no attention to them. They do not mourn or wail for them. They even go away from a battlefield, leaving their fallen friends on the ground. Then there are no days of mourning for them."

Now the white army officers and government agents wanted all Indians to live on reservations and give up their tribal life. The Indians, who had never known exact boundaries around their own lands, were to live in one certain place and raise crops and cattle. They would have to give up hunting the buffalo and other animals. If they did this, the great white Father — or the Grandfather, as the Indians often called the president — would give them seeds for crops and a few cattle to start their herds. The Indians would be safe from soldiers forever, they were promised.

However, most reservations were on sandy, scrubby land that was unfit for farming. To the Sioux, reservation life was the same as prison. When some gave in and settled on the reservations, they were looked down on by other Sioux. But to the whites, the liberty-loving, hunting Sioux who refused farm life became enemies or "hostiles."

From 1860 to 1864 there were fewer bluecoat soldiers on the Plains. The regular United States army was needed in the Civil War when whites were fighting whites. Sitting Bull was almost ready to sign a peace treaty if whites would allow the Sioux to keep their holy land, the Black Hills, and enough of the Plains for buffalo hunts.

And then, one cold day in the winter of 1864-1865, a tired, half-frozen messenger plodded through the snow to Sitting Bull. His message came from the Cheyenne tribe, who were old friends of the Sioux. The Cheyennes under chiefs Black Kettle and White Antelope, the message said, had smoked the peace pipe with the whites at Fort Lyon, in southeast Colorado. The Cheyennes had then set up a camp on Sand Creek, not far from the fort. Some of their men went hunting, leaving about three hundred people in camp, mostly women and children. The camp had suddenly been attacked by a bluecoat army of one thousand, under orders from a Colonel Chivington to kill as many Indians as possible, even the children.

The surprised, unarmed Indians gathered under a United States flag, begging for mercy. But they were shot down by the white soldiers, many seemingly gone mad like their commander. Some of the attacking soldiers had shot into the air so as not to hurt the Indians. But nevertheless, 105 Indian women and children and 28 men were killed. Black Kettle escaped. White Antelope died from the bluecoats' bullets, singing his death song:

> Nothing lives long
> Only earth and mountains.

Two years before, there had been an uprising of eastern Sioux on their Minnesota reservation. Angered by having their reservation land reduced to half its size and by not receiving promised rations, the Minnesota Sioux murdered more than 350 white settlers. The western or Teton Sioux had nothing to do with the massacre. But it had a part in causing some whites to vow death to all Indians, as was proved in the Sand Creek massacre.

On the wintry day of the Cheyenne's visit, Sitting Bull listened in anger. When the messenger took out his pipe and asked Sitting Bull to join in a war against the whites, Sitting Bull agreed to smoke the war pipe. He said then, as he was to say again many times, "White men are liars, thieves, and murderers. They break treaties; they steal our land; they murder women and children." So it was that in 1865 the Plains Indians declared war on the whites. Eight thousand troops were sent from the Union Army at the end of the Civil War, to fight Indians in the West.

Sitting Bull now rode out almost daily to fight the white men who were still pouring into the Plains. The Indians lay in wait for wagon trains creaking through their lands. They shot at the "prairie schooners" from behind rocks in mountain passes. They attacked the wagons drawn up in circles for rest, galloping around and around them, war whooping and shooting arrows and guns as white men and women fired back. But still the white people came, new trails were opened, and land west of the Plains became settled. When gold was discovered in Montana, groups of miners joined the settlers going west.

In 1867, the white men began a new and strange activity. They built a road through Sioux country, first laying short logs crosswise on the trail, then pounding down long iron rails across the logs. The Indians, of course, tore up logs and rails whenever possible, though bluecoats guarded the new roads. Finally, great wagons on iron wheels appeared on the rails, blowing out fire and hot smoke.

These wagons carried not only people but also food and supplies. The Indians attacked the trains, too, and seized the freight loads when they could. The trains scared away buffalo and game. In fact, some whites shot at buffalo from train windows, just "for fun."

Sitting Bull led his Hunkpapas in raid after raid, and he sang his own war songs during the battles. He would chant:

  No chance for me to live;
  Mother, you may as well mourn me.

Her Holy Door did not like this. She told Sitting Bull, "Be more careful in battle. Pity me. If you are killed, it will be hard on me and your whole family." Sitting Bull, at thirty-four, had a large family — two wives and three children. Indians might have as many wives as they wished, as long as they could support them. It would indeed be difficult for his family if Sitting Bull were killed, so Sitting Bull stopped singing his mother song, and sang,

>Friends, I am a soldier
>And have many people
>Jealous of me.

Meanwhile, some of the Hunkpapas were not satisfied with their old leaders. For many years they had had four chiefs leading the tribe. Now they decided that the band would be better off with only one chief, and they chose Four Horns, Sitting Bull's uncle, to be their leader.

Four Horns, however, thought that the Hunkpapas should have a younger chief, and he wanted this to be his nephew, Sitting Bull. The old chief stood before the high council and told of Sitting Bull's outstanding record. Sitting Bull was brave and had been twice wounded, laming him for life. He never quarreled with his own people. He was generous, giving away horses he had captured, and sharing with the poor the game he killed. He was a singer and maker of songs, and a good speaker. He was also a medicine man who was close to Wakan Tanka and who could foretell the future. He led the Midnight Strong Hearts, who struck terror in all enemies. And he had pledged to hold Hunkpapa land against all whites.

So Sitting Bull was elected chief of the Hunkpapas without one vote against him. With Wakan Tanka's help, he hoped to restore Hunkpapa land to its owners and bring peace to the Plains.

CHAPTER VI

Electing a Chief of All the Plains Sioux

The war with the whites went on and on. United States army officers tried to make further treaties with the Indians. But most Indians remembered the broken Treaty of 1851 and laughed at white promises which meant nothing. Finally the Teton Sioux decided to join all its bands together under one chief. And so, in 1868, they all gathered in five great camps along the Missouri River near Standing Rock, in the Sioux's Dakota reservation. A great lodge was built for the council meeting of the Sioux's head men, where Sitting Bull was elected chief of all the Plains Sioux. Crazy Horse, the young Oglala chief, was chosen to be second in command.

Sitting Bull was grateful for the honor paid to him, but he well knew the tremendous responsibility he now had. The good of the whole Sioux nation rested on his shoulders. He was the one to decide how the Indians should deal with the whites. The soldiers seemed anxious to end the fighting, and Sitting Bull felt that the Sioux might be able to keep their land by an agreement with the white men.

And so Sitting Bull announced his peace terms for the whites: 1. Close the white men's roads through Sioux lands. 2. Burn down the forts on Sioux land. 3. Stop the steamboats on Sioux rivers. 4. Send away all white settlers except traders.

Peace commissioners from Washington came and went, but all tried to get the Indians to sign a treaty that would eventually mean reservation living. If the Sioux signed, they promised, the government would see that they would never want for food, clothes, or shelter. Sitting Bull refused to have anything to do with any officials as long as whites were invading land belonging to the Indians.

Meanwhile, fighting continued. Sitting Bull made up a song to the young Sioux braves:

> Young men, help me, please help me.
> I love my country
> That is why I am fighting.

Finally, in the spring of 1868, a commission agreed to let the missionary, Father Pierre Jean De Smet, try to make peace with the Sioux and Sitting Bull. Father De Smet — "Black Robe" to the Indians — was a Jesuit missionary. He had built one mission twenty-seven years before, in the Montana wilderness, and later, another. Now sixty-seven years old, he went to Fort Rice on the Dakota reservation with Major Charles Galpin, a white trader, and his Indian wife who interpreted for the men. These white men were two people whom Sitting Bull trusted.

This spring Sitting Bull was camped on the Powder River in Montana. When runners brought word that these three wanted to visit him he said he would welcome them. He sent eighteen braves back to Fort Rice with the runners, to escort the guests to the Hunkpapas. And he moved his whole camp four miles to the fork of the Powder and Yellowstone rivers. Six hundred tepees made the great circle.

The journey to the Hunkpapas in his carriage took Father De Smet over two weeks. But it was a pleasant trip. Spring flowers dotted the prairie and mountains. Trees on the hills wore their new dresses of pale green. Birds sang. Whites and Indians were happy in spring. All were tired of bloodshed.

On June 18, 1868, scouts' mirrors flashed sun signals to Sitting Bull. Black Robe with a large company of Indians was nearing the Hunkpapas. So Sitting Bull himself, with Four Horns, Black Moon, Gall, Bull Owl, and four hundred other warriors, met the visitors a few miles from the settlement. When they finally arrived at camp, the guests were almost overwhelmed by five thousand Indians swarming to welcome them with songs and gifts.

Sitting Bull led the three visitors to the lodge in the camp's center. He gave them food, water, and more gifts. Later, Sitting Bull and Black Robe talked far into the night.

The next morning a council was held in a great, newly built leaf arbor with leather sides. It covered a half-acre. It was big enough to hold the whole camp of men, women, and children who had come to hear their friend, Black Robe.

First, warriors sang and danced. Then the peace pipe was smoked. Finally Black Moon stood and addressed the missionary, ending with, "Speak, Black Robe. Our ears are open."

Black Robe began with a prayer. He went on, "This cruel war must be stopped. I beg you, forget the past, accept this offering of peace." After a few more words, he sat down.

Black Moon again spoke, followed by Sitting Bull. Major Galpin wrote the speeches as they were given, word for word. This was the first time Sitting Bull's actual words were written while he spoke them. Sitting Bull thanked

Possibly the first photograph taken of Sitting Bull, by O. S. Goff in 1881

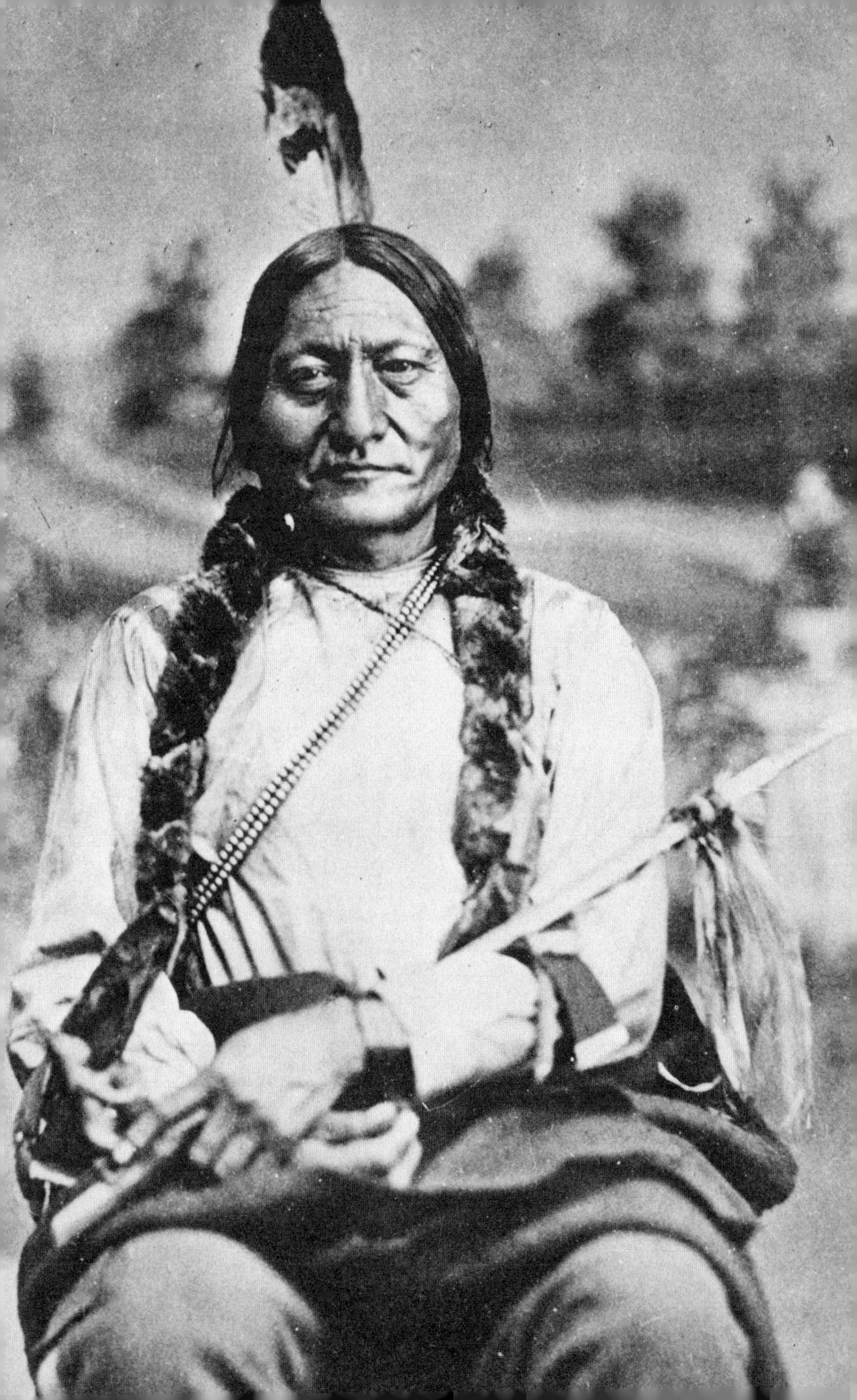

Father De Smet for his prayers, and said, "Welcome, Father, messenger of peace. . . . I hope quiet will be restored. My people will meet chiefs of the Great Father. I hope peace will be made. Then I will be the friend of whites." Then he asked the great listening crowd, "Did you hear my words?"

The Indians cried, approving, "Hau! Hau! Hau!"

But Sitting Bull had more to say. "I forgot two things. 1. I will not sell any part of my country nor let whites cut timber on it, especially oak. 2. Forts full of white soldiers must be abandoned. They are the greatest cause of trouble to my people."

Father De Smet agreed to report Sitting Bull's words to United States peace commissioners. Sitting Bull send Gall, Bull Owl, and Running Antelope to sign a treaty for him, if his terms were approved. The treaty *was* accepted in Fort Rice and signed by Sitting Bull's braves. The same terms were accepted in Laramie where the broken Treaty of 1851 had been signed seventeen years before.

The Treaty of 1868 promised that "the country west of the Missouri River, north of the North Platte River, east of the summit of the Big Horn Mountains" would belong to the Indians. The holy Black Hills were in this country. Any forts there would be abandoned and the roads would be closed. Furthermore, the Sioux might hunt buffalo on any lands north of the North Platte in or outside the above boundaries. The treaty also promised that no future treaty could be made unless signed by three-fourths of all Sioux men.

Sitting Bull had ended the Sioux war with the white people. Or had he? Could whites ever be trusted by red men? Sitting Bull was not sure.

CHAPTER VII

More Broken Promises

With peace restored, Sitting Bull now had time to work on the picture story of his life. He painted the pictures on sheets of buffalo hide, beginning with his first coup as a boy of fourteen. Most of the pictures or pictographs showed him in battle, seated on his war horse. Each painting had a thin line drawn from Sitting Bull's mouth to his mark in an upper corner — the picture of a buffalo bull, sitting up. There were sixty-three pictures of his coups or brave deeds, covering his life up to the year 1870. In that year, they were stolen by a white man. Sitting Bull had no heart to start all over again with other pictures.

However, Chief Four Horns had made copies of forty of his nephew's pictures. These copies are now in Washington, D.C., in the archives of the Bureau of American Ethnology — where records of the early Americans are kept.

The Sioux, at peace with the whites, went back to their buffalo hunts and old wars with the Crows. One day in snowy January, 1869, the Tree Popping Moon, Sitting Bull came upon some of his braves wrestling with a Pony Express rider, Frank Grouard. Frank wore a big, shaggy buffalo-skin coat which two of the Sioux wanted. Sitting Bull stopped the fight and at once adopted Frank. The Sioux called the rider Hands Up or Bear because his coat made him look like a great bear. But six years later Bear deserted the Sioux and became a scout for the white soldiers. Then the Indians called him "Turncoat."

At this time, Indian chiefs were often invited to Washington to meet the president and officials, in hopes of reaching a better understanding between whites and Indians. However, when Sitting Bull was invited to Washington, he answered, "I am too busy. I must stay with my people."

The peace of 1868 did not last long. White settlers still lived on Sioux land. Then white men heard rumors of gold in the Black Hills and began seeking it on Indian land. The new Northern Pacific Railroad was begun along the Yellowstone River in Sioux territory.

One day in 1872, Sitting Bull and a party of Indians came upon a camp of white soldiers on Sioux land. As the Indians drew near, the soldiers fired upon them. A battle was started, lasting all morning, with neither side gaining any ground. Finally, tired of aimless shooting and yelling,

Painting on buffalo skin by Sitting Bull

43 MORE BROKEN PROMISES

Sitting Bull, carrying only his pipe, calmly walked toward the United States soldiers. Then he sat down in the grass facing them, perhaps one hundred yards away. He took out flint and steel, struck fire and lit his pipe, and puffed away. Once he turned his head to call to his braves, "Any wishing to smoke with me, come!"

Sitting Bull's nephew White Bull and another young brave, Gets the Best of Them, walked to Sitting Bull and sat down beside him. Two Cheyennes followed. Sitting Bull then handed his pipe down the line for each to puff. When it was passed back to him, he took out a sharp stick for a pipe cleaner, cleared ashes from the pipe bowl, stood up and walked slowly away. All the time, soldiers' bullets kicked up the dust around them, but hit none of the five warriors. This is perhaps the best remembered of Sitting Bull's brave actions.

By 1875, everyone knew that the 1868 treaty had been so often broken by the whites that it was useless. Troops of soldiers openly scouted the sacred Black Hills, planning to set up a post in those mountains. Heading a troop of the United States Seventh Cavalry into the Hills was Colonel George Armstrong Custer. Colonel Custer had been a hero of the Civil War. Brave and reckless, he had led his men from victory to victory, and was promoted again and again until he became a "brevet" general, a rank to be held only until the war ended. He was the youngest general in the Union Army. People called him the "boy general with golden curls," because of his long curly blond hair. Eleven horses were shot under him but the young officer himself received only one slight wound. "Custer's luck" seemed to give him a charmed life.

At the war's end, it was General Custer who received the flag of truce from Confederate General Robert E. Lee at Appomattox Courthouse in Virginia. After the war, Custer's rank fell from brevet general to lieutenant colonel in the regular army. Custer, disappointed in his loss of rank, was eager to work up again to the top. He would stop at nothing to become a general, it was said. After that, what would keep him from higher rank — even that of president?

When Long Hair Custer, as the Indians called him, returned from scouting the Black Hills, he reported that they held much gold. He showed gold nuggets to prove it. Now all the good work of the United States Indian Bureau during the past thirty years was undone. Nothing could stop a gold rush through the Hills' beautiful fir trees. The Indians called the whites' road into the Black Hills the "Thieves' Road."

Sitting Bull kept his people away from the whites invading their country as long as possible. Then a commission tried to buy the Black Hills from the Sioux. "We want no white men here," Sitting Bull told the government officials. "The Black Hills belong to us. If the whites try to take them, we will fight."

It was no use; in December, 1875, the Moon of Frost in the Tepee, a government ruling came to the Standing Rock Reservation. It ordered all Sioux to report to the reservation by January 31, 1876.

That winter the Hunkpapas with many other Sioux were camped on the Powder River in Montana, 240 miles from Standing Rock. It was the coldest winter in man's memory. And it was impossible to move a camp anywhere with women and children, through blizzards and snowdrifts often higher than their heads. Again the palefaces had broken their word, this time giving an unlawful command impossible to obey.

Sitting Bull at once sent runners to all Indians west of the Missouri River. His messengers reported Sitting Bull's words, "It is war. Warriors, come to my camp in spring, at the Big Bend of the Rosebud River. We must have one big fight with the soldiers."

At the new council, Sitting Bull was again chosen chief of all the Sioux. He made another new song:

> You tribes, what are you saying?
> I have been a war chief.
> All the same, I am still living.

By June, 1876, Sitting Bull had gathered together the largest meeting of Sioux and their allies ever known. They held the Sun Dance in which Sitting Bull himself danced again for a day and night, until noon of a second day. This he did with blood running down his arms, for fifty tiny bits of flesh had been cut from each arm as his sacrifice to the sun. While he danced, a vision came to him.

Afterwards, he told his vision to all. "I looked up," he said, "and saw soldiers dropping from the sky, like grasshoppers, heads down and hats off, and falling into our camp." The soldiers falling head down meant they were dead. The vision foretold a great Indian victory.

The Sioux thought that soon their troubles would be over. Sitting Bull had foretold it! But Sitting Bull, unsmiling, prayed to Wakan Tanka that the victory would be a lasting one. Would one battle be enough to drive the bluecoats away forever?

CHAPTER VIII

Custer's Last Battle

A few days after Sitting Bull's vision, an army under Colonel George "Three Stars" Crook moved toward the Rosebud River in Montana. There, 1,000 soldiers with 260 Indian scouts fought Sitting Bull's army of probably less than 1,000. After a day's bloody battle, the bluecoats were defeated.

But this was not yet Sitting Bull's victory dream. In his vision all the soldiers fell dead into his camp from a clear sky, not after long fighting.

Sitting Bull now ordered the Indian camp moved west to the Little Big Horn River where hunting was better. It was the largest Indian camp ever brought together on the North American continent. Seven camp circles of different Indian bands covered four miles of the plain on the river's west bank. It is said that two to four thousand warriors were there with several times that number of women and children. And so, over ten thousand Indians sang and rejoiced in this great gathering before the victory promised in Sitting Bull's vision.

Across the winding river were bluffs and ridges broken by narrow ravines. Would the white soldiers fall from over there into the camp on the river plain?

47 CUSTER'S LAST BATTLE

On the night of June 24, 1876, Sitting Bull left his tepee to limp up a low hill near his camp. As always before battle, he prayed to Wakan Tanka to spare his warriors in the fight that he expected.

The next morning, June 25, 1876, women were digging wild turnips in nearby fields above the camp. Suddenly, they saw a cloud of dust in the distance. Bluecoats were coming! Also that morning, two boys roaming the prairie saw a troop of United States cavalry. One boy was killed by the soldiers, but the other escaped to give the alarm at camp. The Indians knew the soldiers were coming. But suddenly, about 125 soldiers galloped into the south end of camp from a hideout in a cottonwood forest. Two alarms had been given, but this surprise attack came from a different direction. These soldiers had not been seen by either the women or the boy.

At once, the war cry rang out along the four-mile camp, "Hoka-hey!" Eagle-bone whistles carried the call to battle. Women and boys ran to bring the war ponies to the men. The warriors dashed for their weapons and leaped on their horses. Between war whoops they shouted, "Today is a good day to die!"

Sitting Bull went to his lodge for weapons as his horse was brought to him. He ordered women and children to flee to safety and he galloped off to the fight.

The bluecoat horse soldiers, headed by Major Marcus Reno, were already firing into the Hunkpapa camp when the first warriors clashed with them. Gall's tepee was destroyed and his whole family killed. Gall, in a frenzy, led the charge against the attackers.

Now, to his surprise, Sitting Bull saw Reno's men leap

from their horses to fight on foot. Why didn't they follow up their first attack and charge on? Why dismount when they were so badly outnumbered?

There could be but one answer, Sitting Bull decided — other bluecoats in greater numbers must be very near, as reinforcements. Quickly, Sitting Bull sent scouts in all directions, to locate the other enemy troops that had been seen by the women and boy and must be so close. But no more soldiers came in time to help Major Reno. He was soon hemmed in on all sides but the river. The cavalry mounted again, to retreat. Surrounded on three sides, the soldiers made for the river. Those who were left crossed the Little Big Horn and climbed the bluff on the other side. On top of the bluff, they began digging in, to escape the deadly hail of bullets and arrows.

Major Reno's help did not come until late afternoon, and by that time he had lost about one-third of his men. Then Captain Frederick Benteen arrived with more cavalry, on the craggy side of the river. They had been slowed by rough going through the Badlands. Even though he brought as many men as Major Reno had, there were still not enough to turn the battle. They, too, were trapped and dug in beside Reno's men.

But before the Benteen troops arrived, a greater battle was being fought at the other end of the camp, out of sight of those on the bluff at the south. Sitting Bull had seen a column of dust billowing toward the ridges opposite the south tepees, and ordered other warriors to lie in wait for this new force of cavalry. The Indians did not know until afterward that this column of more than two hundred soldiers was headed by Colonel George Armstrong Custer.

He had been stationed at Fort Abraham Lincoln, across the Missouri River from Bismarck, North Dakota.

With the colonel were his two younger brothers, a brother-in-law, and a seventeen-year-old nephew. They were all counting on the Custer luck to take part in a great victory, which might lead to a President Custer of the United States.

His scouts had warned the colonel of this greatest of all Indian camps. They advised against attacking it with so few men. But Colonel Custer saw that his victory would be all the greater if it were against great odds.

As quietly as possible, the Custer division of the Seventh United States Cavalry rode two by two over the hills across the river from the north part of the camp. Colonel Custer's red and blue forked pennant, with crossed white swords and the number "7" above them, waved at the head of the troops. Shaking off biting mosquitoes and buffalo gnats, and trusting their horses to bypass rattlesnakes and gopher holes, the young men cantered toward their doom. They had not seen the Reno division, almost four miles away. It was the early afternoon of Sunday, June 25, 1876.

The Indian camp was larger than Custer had expected. The day was terribly hot, his tired men choked in the dust and were sweating through their heavy blue uniforms. Wild roses and bright loco flowers decorating the horses had wilted. But the men sat their horses grimly, ready to charge the first enemy in sight. The order came to ford the river and to make a "surprise" attack on the camp on the other side.

And then the shrill war cry, "Hoka-hey!" screamed into the soldiers' ears from all sides. No one had seen Crazy

Horse's braves hiding in a ravine behind them. Suddenly the soldiers were surrounded by Indians leaping from the ravine and by others led by Gall splashing across the ford to meet them. The Seventh Cavalry was forced to back out of the ford and mount the hill behind them.

On the hilltop, Custer's troops bunched up around him, fighting bravely to the end. Some Indians fell, pierced by bullets or falling under bayonets. Soldiers fell under bullets, arrows, clubs, knives, and spears. In a half hour, it was said, not one cavalry man was left alive. Long Hair Custer, at thirty-seven, lay dead on top of the hill, surrounded by his officers and men. His four young relatives lay dead, too. Custer's luck had deserted them all.

A few days later, the only living thing that survived Custer's last stand was found roaming near the battlefield: an officer's wounded sorrel war horse, Comanche. The reddish brown animal's wounds soon healed and it became the mascot of the Seventh Cavalry. Comanche, his saddle empty, was led in all the cavalry parades for many years. Its stirrups always held empty cavalry boots pointing backward, in memory of Custer's last stand.

Sitting Bull had galloped up from directing the other battle and guarding women and children to see the Custer fight. "All are dead?" he asked when he had crossed the river.

"All are dead," came the answer.

But Sitting Bull was not happy. "Attend to our dead," he ordered. "Four days of mourning for the losses of our slain must pass before rejoicing. We should also mourn the bluecoats who fought so bravely." Then, "Make ready to break camp tomorrow," he went on. "Too many died." And again he climbed a hill, praying to Wakan Tanka for wisdom to lead his people.

The next morning young braves were still surrounding the Reno and Benteen troops. The Indians wanted to wipe them out as the Custer troops had been wiped out. But at noon Sitting Bull ordered an end with, "Henala! — Enough! Enough of killing. Break camp at once. Let each band return to its own hunting ground."

Finally the Indian leaders began to understand Sitting Bull's sadness. With complete destruction of the Seventh Cavalry's finest men, the whole United States army would be aroused against the Indians as never before. How would it all end?

That Monday afternoon, the day after their victory, with their dead hidden in caves or under rock piles, the Indians marched away from the Little Big Horn camp. Men, women, and children, horses and dogs, made a line three miles long and one-half mile wide. In the Big Horn Mountains, the bands would spread out, seeking wider hunting grounds.

On Tuesday, June 27, 1876, the troops of General Alfred Terry arrived at Custer's Hill. The general had expected to join Custer, Reno, and Benteen in surrounding and attacking the Indian camp. Instead, his soldiers must bury their dead comrades. Most of the dead had nothing to show who they were. They were buried together in trenches. Colonel Custer's body, however, was recognized. Along with 38 of Reno's wounded, all were carried on horse litters 53 miles to the steamboat "Far West" on the Yellowstone River. They went 710 miles by the boat down the Yellowstone to Bismarck, on the Missouri River. From there Custer's body was finally taken to West Point to be buried. Altogether, 205 men had died with Custer on the hill, plus about 60 more of the Reno troops.

The Indians claimed only 32 warriors lost, besides Gall's wife and children, the only family said to have been killed in the fighting.

When news of Custer's defeat finally reached the East, the nation was angry as it had not been since Civil War days. All Indians must die or live on reservations, people said. Some people called the Custer battle a "massacre," but they were wrong, for the cavalry had attacked first and was well-armed. The cavalry's plan to attack from two sides at once and then surround the Indians had failed, mainly because the officers did not believe reports of the Indians' great numbers. Their scouts' warnings had been in vain.

This was the greatest victory ever won by North American Indians over United States troops. But Sitting Bull worried and wondered. Had he won a battle and lost a war?

CHAPTER IX

Trails to the Four Winds

Soon after Custer's last stand, the Sioux realized that again their great chief had known their future. The army wanted revenge for the Custer defeat, and soldiers began pouring by the thousands onto the Great Plains. They came on foot and on horseback, and were armed with the most deadly rifles and the biggest cannon yet seen by Indians. The army was to stay until all Sioux were either destroyed or living on reservations.

Sioux reservations were mainly in North and South Dakota. Each reservation had an agent, who was sent from Washington to manage it. These officers were stationed at small settlements with a store and a few houses for the agent, his helpers, and the police, who were usually Indians from enemy tribes of the Sioux. They often wore metal shields on their chests, so the Sioux called them "Metal Breasts."

Appointments of agents often depended on politics. When the agents came west, many knew nothing about Indians or how to deal with them. Sometimes the agents were dishonest and cheated the Indians of their land and food rations. No wonder that the Sioux — the fighting men — refused to live on reservations until hunting was almost at an end.

After Custer's defeat, the army came to punish not only the hunting Indians, or "hostiles," but also reservation Indians. The army declared that the Sioux had broken their peace treaty. Yet it was the army that had attacked the Indian camp.

The reservation Indians were ordered to give up their horses and their guns. The horses then might be given to Pawnee policemen. Pawnees were the Sioux's worst Indian enemies.

After the great Indian meeting on the Little Big Horn River, food became scarce. There were too many people to feed in the Big Horn Mountains where hunting now was poor. Yet Sitting Bull went on keeping his Hunkpapas away from the armies. He stayed in the mountains instead of risking them on the Plains where a few buffalo might still be found. More war with the palefaces might end in the Sioux's destruction. Sitting Bull's Indians spent all that summer of 1876 dodging troops and hunting with little success.

Sitting Bull began to think of moving to Canada, to escape the bluecoats and starvation.

In September, 1876, a peaceful gathering of reservation men, women, and children at Slim Buttes, South Dakota, was attacked by General Crook. Sitting Bull led his Sioux warriors to the place but arrived too late to save the Indians.

In October, Colonel Nelson Miles started to build a fort on Sioux land at the fork of the Yellowstone and Tongue rivers. Hunkpapa warriors under Gall, angered at this invasion of land belonging to the Indians, attacked a wagon train nearing the new fort and drove off forty-seven mules. The rest of the wagon train was forced to return to the supply base for more mules and soldiers to protect them. The second train, fighting off more attacks, got safely through. As white reserves kept coming on in greater numbers against the dwindling group of Indians, Sitting Bull saw that they must try to reach an agreement.

And so the chief of the Sioux sent for Big Leggings Brughiére, a half-breed in the Hunkpapa band. Big Leggings could read and write English, as Sitting Bull could not, since Sitting Bull refused to learn the hated white man's language. He told Big Leggings what to write in a note to the white soldiers:

I want to know what you are doing on this road. You scare all the buffaloes away. I want to hunt in this place. I want you to turn back from here. If you don't, I will fight you again. I want you to leave what you have got here and turn back from here.

I am your friend,
Sitting Bull

After his name came a postscript with the most important part of his letter:

I mean all the rations you have got and some powder.

The note was left in a forked stick on a path near the soldiers' camp. It was soon found and given to Colonel E. S. Otis.

The colonel's curt answer was that he would keep on taking supplies to the new fort and would fight the Indians any time they tried to stop him.

Then Sitting Bull was angrier than ever. But some of his followers persuaded him to meet with Colonel Miles, who was camped only four miles away. At first there was trouble in deciding upon a meeting place, for neither leader would go to the other's camp. Finally Sitting Bull promised to meet the colonel halfway between the camps in an open space in the forest. Soldiers and warriors accompanying their leaders were to be unarmed.

Sitting Bull took four chiefs and two hundred warriors with him. Two of the chiefs were his nephew White Bull and his adopted brother, Jumping Bull. Colonel Miles also came with a small army. Sitting Bull and his chiefs sat on a buffalo robe, and Colonel Miles and his officers sat opposite them. The Indians called the colonel "Bear Coat" because he wore a long, heavy coat trimmed with bear fur. Big Leggings Brughiére sat between the two leaders, to interpret.

All that day the leaders talked. Once Sitting Bull said, "All I want is to find more meat for my people."

Bear Coat replied, "Sitting Bull, now you are hunting. But some day you will have an agency all your own to live on."

The chief and the colonel were polite to each other. But they settled nothing that day. The next day they met again. This time, Bear Coat became angry when Sitting Bull still refused to give up his old way of life and live on a reservation. The meeting broke up shortly, with no peace pipe smoked. Suddenly, in a rage, Colonel Miles told Sitting Bull, "I will give you fifteen minutes to leave this place or my men will fire on you!" It was one of the greatest insults possible — as if a Sioux would run from attack! And weren't the soldiers supposed to have come unarmed?

Big Leggings was not a good interpreter. He either did not tell Sitting Bull these words, or the chief misunderstood. Or perhaps Bear Coat Miles ordered his men to fire before the time was up. At any rate, the Indians were completely surprised when a volley of gun fire suddenly blasted at them. One Sioux was killed and another wounded during the short skirmish that followed, before both sides returned to their camps.

The next day the battle continued. But the white troops brought their artillery into action. Indians could not fight against cannon, even these small ones mounted on wheels. So they began a retreat of forty miles into deeper forest. Then, worn and starving, two thousand of the Indians surrendered, agreeing to march to an agency under army escort. Colonel Miles was satisfied. But Sitting Bull, Gall, and Crazy Horse continued to lead the remainder of their followers as before. Jumping Bull was always near his chief.

By now the hunting grounds were so diminished that not enough game was left to feed even this smaller band of Indians. Some of them began to steal away, a few at a time, to the reservations where they were promised food. Yet hundreds of Sitting Bull's most loyal followers refused to surrender.

Meanwhile, another treaty was declared by the United States government, giving the Black Hills and Powder River country to the whites. It was signed by a few chiefs on reservations, though the 1868 treaty had stated that three-fourths of the Indian men must sign such a treaty. Those who signed said they did so because their people were already starving on the reservations. Agents had declared that no rations would be given out until the treaty was signed.

It was a hard winter for the hunting Sioux, and Sitting

Bull decided that they should move north to Canada in the spring. Crazy Horse and Gall wanted to stay on their own hunting grounds. Finally, Gall did go to Canada, and by spring, Crazy Horse surrendered his nine hundred starving Oglalas to the white men. He was promised a reservation for them on the Powder River.

The following September, 1877, Crazy Horse was taken by soldiers to Fort Robinson in northwest Nebraska. He was told that General Crook wanted to see him there. But when he arrived, two Indian policemen, one on either side, started leading him toward the guardhouse. Crazy Horse knew then that he was to be jailed, and tried to get away. At that, a bluecoat stabbed him in the back with his bayonet and Crazy Horse died, thirty-five years old.

In May, Moon of Wild Strawberries, 1877, Sitting Bull had led the last of his Hunkpapas two hundred miles north into Canada, the land of the Grandmother, Queen Victoria. The Canadian redcoat soldiers did not kill Indians as did the bluecoats, the chief told his people.

Once in Canada, the redcoats made Sitting Bull promise only three things: 1. No horse stealing. 2. No raiding Americans across the border. 3. Sitting Bull must control his own young men, and punish them if they broke any law. Sitting Bull had hoped for a reservation in Canada for his people. But he was not a Canadian and there was no reservation for him.

The Hunkpapas stayed in Canada for four years, and lived in peace.

For awhile there was food enough for all. In 1878, Sir John MacDonald, Canada's Minister of the Interior, wrote, "The Sioux have behaved remarkably well ever since they crossed the Canadian border." But soon, times changed. Winters were long, and drought burned crops the Sioux planted. Game grew scarce. There were even fewer buffalo herds in Canada than there now were in the United States. Against the law, Indians began crossing the border to hunt buffalo. By 1881, the Hunkpapas were again beginning to starve.

The Canadian government did not have enough food for the strangers in time of famine, and so it asked the United States to take them back. To Sitting Bull's surprise, a United States commission under General Terry — the same general who had come to Custer's Hill after the battle — came to see him in Canada. The general asked Sitting Bull to return to the United States, with all his wars "forgiven."

Sitting Bull answered, "If there is one white man who speaks truth, send him to me. I will listen. I don't believe in governments that made fifty-two treaties with Sioux and broke all." General Terry and his commission went away, disappointed.

Now a large reward was offered for bringing Sitting Bull into the United States. Nobody was able to collect.

All United States reservation Indians had been forced to give up their rifles. Sitting Bull's Sioux still had their guns and horses. Both Canada and the United States feared the Sioux might start another war — even spreading to a war between the United States and Canada. Both countries said that Sitting Bull must go "home."

It was his people's starvation that brought Sitting Bull back. In July, 1881, he arrived on horseback at Fort Buford in the northwest corner of North Dakota. With him was his friend, Jean Louis Le Gare, a Canadian trapper and trader. Forty lodges, about 187 Hunkpapas, followed the chief back to the United States. A few stayed in Canada. For the first time in his life, Sitting Bull surrendered. He expected to be seized and killed as Crazy Horse had been killed.

At the fort, Sitting Bull handed his gun to his eight-year-old son, Crowfoot, to give up. "If you live," the chief told his son sadly, "you will never be a man in the world. For you can never have a pony or a gun."

The Hunkpapas were ordered to Standing Rock Agency at Fort Yates, on the Missouri River. Sitting Bull was taken farther south, down the Missouri to Fort Randall, on South Dakota's southern border. There he was kept as a prisoner

Crowfoot,
Sitting Bull's son

Standing Holy,
Sitting Bull's daughter

of war for two years. He was treated almost as a guest, for he was well-liked by the soldiers, and was visited by friends, reporters, and travelers. Many asked for his autograph. So ten days after his surrender, Sitting Bull, who had never learned to write, was copying his name from a paper given him, printing it in big capitals.

In May, 1883, Sitting Bull was returned to Standing Rock. The Sioux chief and the agent there, Major "White Hair" McLaughlin, disliked each other at sight. Jealous of Sitting Bull's power, the agent gave him "women's work" to do, such as hoeing. But soon Sitting Bull was invited to tour fifteen cities so that people could see the man who had defeated Custer. After that, he agreed to join "Buffalo Bill's Wild West Show."

"Buffalo Bill" was William F. Cody. He had been a pony express rider, scout, and buffalo hunter who provided buffalo meat for railroad workers. He boasted of killing 4,280 buffalo in seventeen months. Later he became a showman, taking his acts all through cities in the eastern United States and Canada. The shows were in circus tents, with such acts as covered wagons chased by Indians in war dress who were shooting blunt arrows and blank cartridges, and Indian horse races. It was all very exciting.

Buffalo Bill often visited the West to get more Indians for his big acts, and he asked Sitting Bull to join him. Bill, killer of buffalo, settler of the West, a scout for Colonel Custer, stood for all the things Sitting Bull hated. Yet the chief admired his daring. The two understood each other and, in 1885, Sitting Bull rode the iron horse on the iron trail east to join the show.

Sitting Bull became the hit of the show. He was introduced to the big audiences as the "Slayer of Custer," which, of course, he was not. At that, onlookers often hissed and catcalled. Sitting Bull paid no attention to anyone as he rode his big gray horse around the ring, his long war bonnet trailing behind him. He put his trained horse through its tricks: at a pistol shot, it sat on its haunches, "shook hands," and rolled over.

Sitting Bull enjoyed the Wild West Show and his many friends in it. He "adopted" Annie Oakley, famous rifle shot in the show, and called her "Sure Shot." But he did not like big cities. He wished he had known sooner how many whites there were, and said, "If every Indian killed one at every step, the dead would not be missed."

Finally he told Buffalo Bill, "I am tired of noise and big buildings. Whites point fingers at me, make faces of hate. They talk all the time, like the noise of waterfalls that go on forever. My people need me at home."

Even the promise of meeting Queen Victoria in England the next year, when the show would play there honoring her fiftieth year on the throne, did not interest Sitting Bull. Buffalo Bill gave him the gray horse when he left, and a big, wide-brimmed hat. And Sitting Bull rode the iron horse home to the Plains.

Whites were now trying to buy reservation land from the Indians. Sitting Bull wanted to stop it. And so Sitting Bull ended his travels to the four winds — north to Canada, then back south to the Plains, east to the big cities, and finally went again, to his people. His cabin in a tiny settlement near the Grand River was on the Standing Rock Reservation in northern South Dakota, not far from the place where he was born.

Sitting Bull with Buffalo Bill

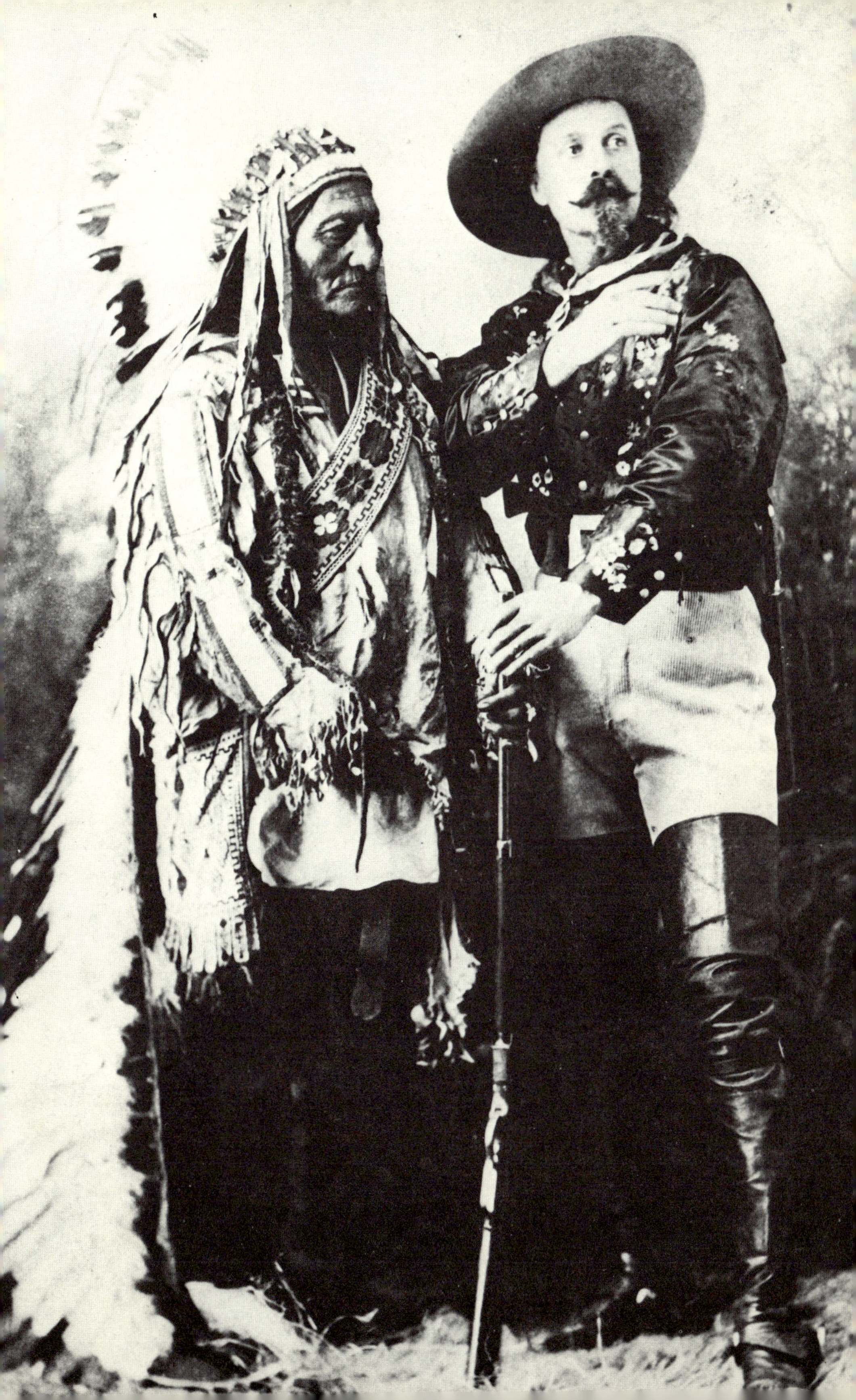

CHAPTER X

Ghosts

Whites were worse than Moon Nibblers, the Mouse Little People who nibbled the moon away, each month, to almost nothing. The white men were now nibbling the Sioux reservations down to a small part of their first size. Each month, the moon grew back again to its full circle. But the reservations did not grow back.

The Sioux reservation had once been a large part of the Dakotas, on both sides of the boundary between the two states. By the time Sitting Bull returned from Canada, it was divided into six separate parts. The Hunkpapas' part was the Standing Rock Agency along the Missouri River on both sides of the state line. But white settlers kept moving west, wanting farm land. And the United States government kept on nibbling at the Sioux reservations, "buying" land from the Indians. Now the Indians were offered fifty cents an acre for Sioux land.

Sitting Bull warned the Hunkpapas not to sell any land at all. He told a government commission, "If a man loses anything and goes back and looks for it, he will find it. That is what the Indians are doing when they ask you to give them the things that were promised in the past."

Gall, who was jealous of Sitting Bull, now became the

favorite of the agent, White Hair McLaughlin. When another commission came to Standing Rock, it offered $1.25 an acre for Sioux land, instead of the fifty cents. Gall and McLaughlin plotted to have the sale signed when Sitting Bull was not there. When the land was sold, Sitting Bull threw up his hands in disgust.

Then one day in October, 1889, Moon of Falling Leaves, a friend named Kicking Bear brought news to Sitting Bull. It had been a hard summer, with a drought that killed all crops. Sitting Bull had foretold the drought and had not even planted any seeds. Then came Kicking Bear with a ray of hope.

The Indians, he said, had a new prophet. His name was Wovoka, and he was a Paiute Indian from western Nevada. The white people called him Jack Wilson. He had been very sick — had, in fact, died and visited the Spirit World and his friends there who had died before him. Then he came back to life with a message from the other world. Soon, perhaps next spring, all dead Indians would come to earth and on a mountain top, meet all Indians who believed in the Spirit. All whites would at once be drowned in a flood below them. And then Indians would live as before whites came, hunting the buffalo and other game, which would be given back to them. To bring this about, Indians must dance the Ghost Dance.

Wovoka's message said,

> All Indians must dance, everywhere, keep on dancing. Soon, next spring, Great Spirit come, bring back game of every kind. . . . All dead Indians come back and live again . . . all strong young men . . . . Old blind Indians see again and get young and have fine

time. When Great Spirit comes, all Indians go to mountains. While Indians up high, big flood comes like water . . . all white people die, get drowned. Then water go away . . . nobody but Indians everywhere . . . game thick. Medicine man tell Indians to keep up dancing and the good times will come. Indians who don't dance, don't believe in this word, will grow little, about a foot high, and stay that way. Some will be turned into wood and be burned in fire!

Sitting Bull did not believe the prophecy. But he welcomed anything bringing cheer to his people. His reservation and others all through the West suddenly became happy places. Everyone danced the Ghost Dance. Sitting Bull danced, too, to please the others.

To dance the Ghost Dance, each dancer usually wore a Ghost Shirt — a long, loose white shirt painted with the sun, moon, stars, eagle, crow, and buffalo. It was said to be bulletproof. The dancers painted their faces red, yellow, green, and blue. They danced in a circle, both men and women, unlike old Indian dances where men and women always danced separately. The dance leaders carried six-foot ghost sticks tipped with red cloth and crow and eagle feathers. They began dancing in mid-afternoon, and might dance all night. By then, many dancers had fainted and fallen to earth. Coming out of a faint, they often claimed to have seen a vision of the new Indian world to come.

As they danced they sang ghost songs, such as,

> The Father says so —
> You shall see your Grandfather
> You shall see your relatives
> The Father says so.

And they prayed,
> Oh, Great Spirit
> Be merciful to me
> That my people may live.

Part of the new religion taught peace, that no Indian should carry a weapon or rise up against the whites. However, the agents saw the Indian Ghost Dancers go mad with excitement over the new world they expected. Agents, government officials, and army officers feared another Indian war if, or when, the prophecy failed to come true. They ordered Ghost Dancing to stop. At Standing Rock, Kicking Bear was ordered to leave, and the agent told Sitting Bull to stop all Ghost Dancing.

Sitting Bull himself stopped dancing, but did not try to make his people stop. A year passed. Some Ghost Dancers had left their farms and crops to live in dancing camps. The spring in which the Great Spirit was to come had gone by, but the dances went on. Sitting Bull finally ordered his followers to stop. For once, he was not obeyed, and United States officials threatened to arrest him for not bringing the dancing to an immediate halt.

Now Buffalo Bill, Sitting Bull's old friend, came to Standing Rock with an order from Colonel Miles to bring the chief to Chicago to meet another commission. The showman arrived at the agency with his wagon loaded with lollipops and other candy to give the Indians. But McLaughlin refused to let Buffalo Bill see Sitting Bull.

Finally, McLaughlin ordered the reservation police to arrest the chief unless the dancing stopped. At that, Crazy Walking, captain of the Indian police, resigned his job. Other Hunkpapas refused to help the Metal Breasts against their beloved chief. But the Ghost Dancers danced on.

Seventh Cavalry troops marched to the Pine Ridge Reservation south of Standing Rock, to try to stop the dances there. Part of the troops headed for Standing Rock and arrived at the agency where friends guarded Sitting Bull in his small settlement of cabins on the Grand River. On the night of December 14, 1890, when friends came to guard his cabin, Sitting Bull sent them away. They needed sleep, he said, after the late Ghost Dance.

Just before dawn, Sitting Bull's cabin was silently surrounded by the Indian police, led by Bull Head. Suddenly they pushed open the door and entered with drawn guns. The chief awoke slowly, dazed by the sudden attack. A match was struck, then a kerosene lamp lit. Two Metal Breasts grabbed Sitting Bull's arms as he sat up and started to dress.

"We are here to arrest you and take you to the agency," Bull Head said.

Red Tomahawk added, "If you fight, we will have to kill you!"

Sitting Bull mumbled sleepily, "Hau — Yes." He went on trying to dress. His wife called to their sons in the next cabin, "Boys, they arrest your father. Saddle the gray horse for him to ride to the agency!"

One son was deaf. Awakened by others in the cabin, he ran to his father. Crowfoot, another son, now seventeen, saddled the circus horse and shouted for help.

Now the whole settlement was aroused. Screaming and war whooping, people came running from all directions. Only one had a rifle which he must have kept hidden when guns were taken from the Indians. He was Catch-the-Bear,

Sitting Bull's chief guard. He shouted, "Where is Bull Head?"

Sitting Bull, fully awake, now shouted, "I will not go!" as he was being dragged from his cabin.

Bull Head tried to quiet his prisoner with, "The agent only wants you to live at the agency. He will treat you well there."

Sitting Bull's adopted brother, Jumping Bull, ran to him, begging, "Brother, let us go to the agency. I go with you. If you die, I die with you."

But the sixty-year-old chief tried to fight off his captors, saying again, "I will not go!"

Then Catch-the-Bear, with the gun, fired at Bull Head in the gray dawn now breaking, and wounded him. As the police leader fell, he fired at Sitting Bull. At the same time, policeman Red Tomahawk fired at Sitting Bull's head, from behind. Either shot would have killed. Sitting Bull, chief of all the Plains Sioux, fell dead.

Bull Head, too, died from his wound. Faithful Jumping Bull died as he had promised, beside his beloved chief, in the fight that followed. Sitting Bull's friends outnumbered

Sitting Bull's house and family, taken the day after he was shot

the police, but the police had rifles. Still, they were no match for the maddened Hunkpapas. The police retreated into the cabin and barred the door after sending one away to Standing Rock to get help from the soldiers. Not until the cavalry arrived did the Metal Breasts escape.

Sitting Bull's seventeen-year-old son Crowfoot was killed by the police, who found him hiding in the cabin. It was to Crowfoot that Sitting Bull had given his gun to surrender on their return from Canada. Then the father had told the eight-year-old boy that, without a gun and horse, he would never be a man.

When the shots first began to ring out, the old circus horse suddenly remembered the tricks he had performed at the sound of a shot. He sat up on his haunches and held out a hoof to shake hands. He rolled over, danced and jumped, and finally ran away across the Plains. The Indians watched in wonder. Some said that Sitting Bull's spirit had entered the gray horse's body and was carried away to the Great Plains he loved.

Later, the gray horse was caught, brought back by Buffalo Bill, and returned to the Wild West Show, where he performed in the Chicago World's Fair of 1893.

Sitting Bull's body was taken to Fort Yates, next to the Standing Rock Agency, and there he was buried. Today a tombstone marks his resting place. On it is carved,

SITTING BULL
Died
Dec. 15, 1890
Chief of the
Hunkpapa
Sioux

CHAPTER XI

After the End

The Sioux did not rise up against the whites after their chief's death, as many had expected. Probably this was because most Indians still believed in the Ghost Dancing. They thought that their Great Spirit would come, bringing back Sitting Bull along with all their other dead.

However, more than 300 Hunkpapas fled the Standing Rock Reservation, fearing punishment for the police killed. Some joined a party of Miniconjou Sioux under Chief Big Foot, seeking a home in the Pine Ridge Reservation in South Dakota's southwest corner. There were about 270 women and children and 100 men in the party.

On December 28, 1890, Seventh Cavalry troops rounding up Indians met the group plodding through the snow, heading for the Pine Ridge Agency to give themselves up. The soldiers had orders to arrest Chief Big Foot, who was already dying of pneumonia. The Indians promised to obey orders and go with the cavalry to the agency the next day.

That snowy night the Indians camped in the snow on Wounded Knee Creek, South Dakota. In the morning the major of the Seventh Cavalry demanded any guns they might have. They had already surrendered all but two guns, but one boy held on to his rifle when asked for it.

He was a deaf mute and did not understand what was going on. When soldiers tried to take the gun from the boy, it went off, probably by accident. The shot started one of the worst massacres ever suffered by Indians at the hands of whites.

The Seventh Cavalry began mowing down the unarmed, screaming women, children, men, and babies. Some wore Ghost Shirts. Thinking the shirts were bulletproof, they did not run away. A few escaped, wading through the snow to caves. Between two and three hundred Indians died in that massacre, while the snow grew red with frozen blood. It was December 29, 1890, just two weeks after the death of Sitting Bull.

Indian Ghost Dances and Indian uprisings were ended. Ghost Shirts had not saved any of their wearers. Sitting Bull, the great Sioux leader, was gone, along with all hope for the Sioux nation.

Now the Sioux settled down on their bits of land in the reservations. Each family was promised 160 acres of farm land, some of the poorest soil in the West. They were given or loaned farm implements and other tools, rations when crops failed, and a few cattle. They hated the cattle and had to learn to eat beef, which at first made some sick. Even the smell of cattle was bad, compared with the fine smell of buffalo.

But wild buffalo herds were gone. Fifty million buffalo are said to have roamed before the white man's coming, but by 1889 there were 541 left. Several years later a few were saved from extinction only by being placed on game reserves safe from any hunter.

The rations of flour and potatoes were also strange to

Chief of all the Plains Sioux,
photographed in 1885

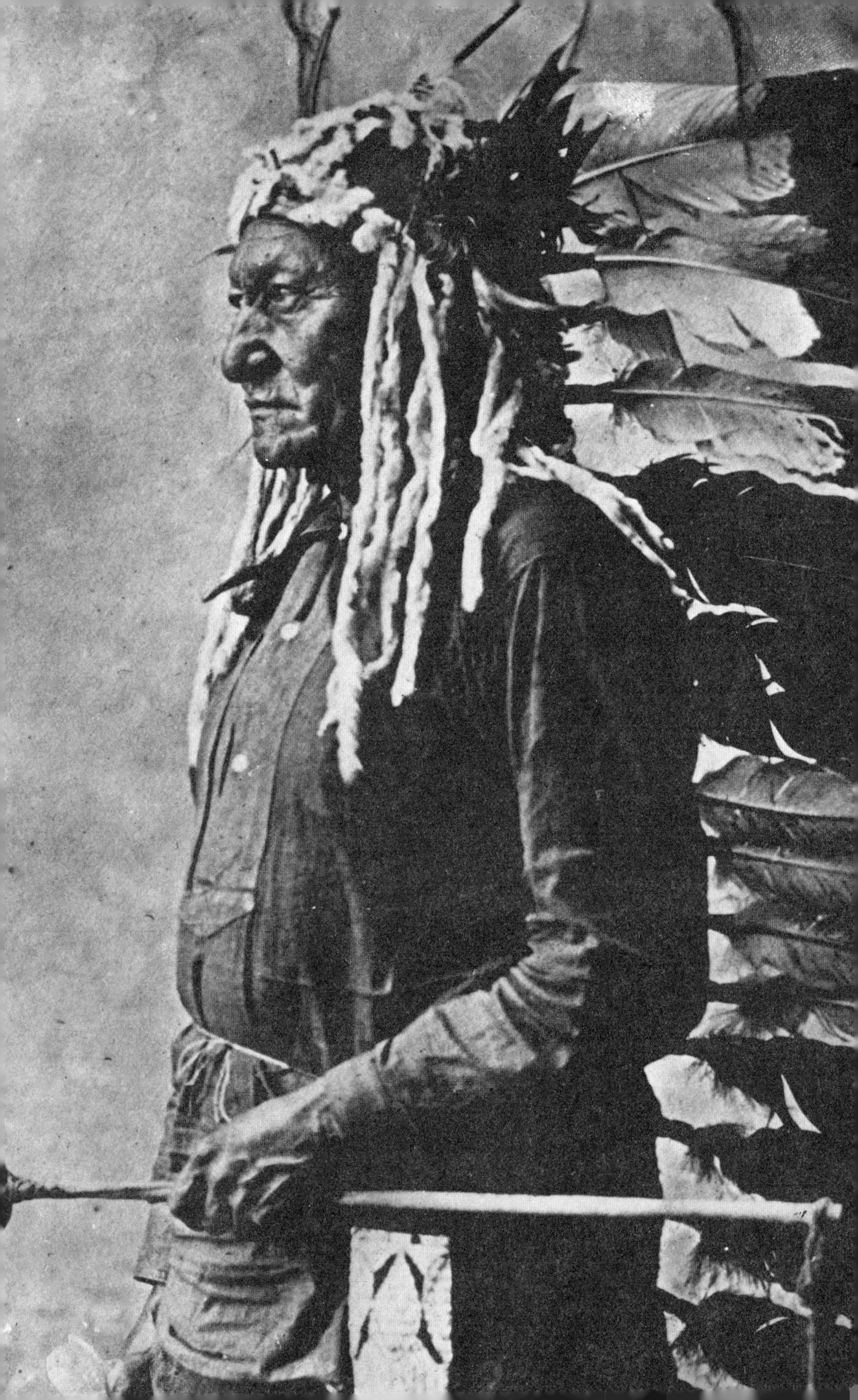

the Indians. At first, not knowing what flour was, they dumped it out and made children's shirts from the sacks.

Yes, the years ahead would be difficult for the Indians. Sitting Bull was among the first to send his children to school — "to learn how to keep from being cheated by the whites." Even today, over seventy-five years later, Indians and whites are still learning how to live together with equal rights.

— — —

And how is Sitting Bull remembered today? He was a warrior and leader of the Strong Hearts, aiming to be always generous and brave, honorable and wise. He was a singer of his own songs and teller of tales, an orator whose people never tired of hearing him. He was an artist in pictograph. He was a fierce foe and a friend to children. He was a medicine man who foretold the future. Sitting Bull was chief of all the Plains Sioux, the only man ever so honored.

THE AUTHOR

A native of Illinois, Faith Yingling Knoop now lives in Little Rock, Arkansas. She taught elementary school after graduating from New Jersey State Teachers College, but for many years her main interest has been writing. She is the author of nine books for young people, including biographies of Balboa, Coronado, and Amerigo Vespucci. Between books, Mrs. Knoop writes short stories and articles for such publications as *Highlights, American Girl,* and *American Junior Red Cross News.* Occasionally, she writes an article for an adult magazine, but she always goes back to the field she likes best — writing for young people. Mrs. Knoop has traveled all over the United States and the world, and has made several visits to the Great Plains area where Sitting Bull lived.

The photographs are reproduced through the courtesy of the Library of Congress, Smithsonian Institution, South Dakota Department of Highways, and South Dakota State Historical Society.

BIOGRAPHIES IN
THIS SERIES ARE

Joseph Brant
Crazy Horse
Geronimo
Chief Joseph
King Philip
Osceola
Powhatan
Red Cloud
Sacajawea
Chief Seattle
Sequoyah
Sitting Bull
Tecumseh
William Warren
William Beltz
Robert Bennett
LaDonna Harris
Oscar Howe
Maria Martinez
Billy Mills
George Morrison
Michael Naranjo
Maria Tallchief
James Thorpe
Pablita Velarde
Annie Wauneka

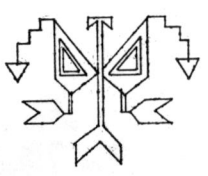

0652 01 083814 01 9 (IC=1)
KNOOP, FAITH YINGLIN 05/25/86
SITTING BULL
(0) C1974 JB SITTING BULL K

J
B   SITTING BULL   209428
KNOOP F
SITTING BULL
                    4.95

DATE DUE		
8/25/78		
7/9/81		

NOV 26 1975

South Huntington Public Library
Huntington Station, New York
11746

005